SHIPWRECKS

SHIPWRECKS

PHILIP S. JENNINGS AND DANY BOSEK

MALLARD PRESS

Page 1: This woodcut from a
Portuguese publication of
1606, *Regimento Nautico,*
reveals that faith in God was
as important as good
seamanship to sailors of an
earlier era.

Pages 2-3: The wrecked car
ferry *Herald of Free Enterprise*
lies on her side in Zeebrugge
harbor. More than 150
people lost their lives in the
disaster in March 1987.

These pages: The steamer
Rhode Island is smashed like a
child's toy off Bonnet Point,
Rhode Island.

CONTENTS

Down in History 6

The Mystery of Missing Ships 18

Collision! 26

Fire Down Below 34

Davy Jones's Locker 42

Steam and Paddle Power 50

Schooners, Brigs, and
Windjammers 64

Poisoned Seas 70

Index and Acknowledgments 80

Down in History

Ask any child or adult on either side of the Atlantic to name the worst sea disaster they ever heard of and it's a fairly safe bet they will name the *Titanic*, a ship which sank eighty years ago. Thus it is impossible for an author examining the tragedy of shipwrecks to omit what remains in American and British hearts and minds as the greatest tragedy of them all. It would be like asking a psychologist to write a book without mentioning Sigmund Freud.

Over the decades speculation as to the whereabouts of the *Titanic* persisted, but it was not until 1985 that a serious search with sophisticated equipment was undertaken by the US Navy research ship *Knorr*. Her cameras were tested on the wreck of a United States nuclear submarine, *Scorpion*, which sank with all hands in 1968. Satisfied with the results, (for security purposes no photographs of the *Scorpion* are available) the *Knorr* set out on her mission.

On 1 September 1985 the *Titanic* was found in 13,000 feet of water. Scientist Robert

Right: The *Olympic*, another great ship of the White Star Line, but one with an active career ahead which was to last into the 1930s.

Below: The undeniable majesty of the *Titanic* in open sea.

WHITE STAR LINE.

TRIPLE-SCREW R.M.S. "OLYMPIC," 46,359 TONS, THE LARGEST BRITISH STEAMER, OFF THE EDDYSTONE LIGHTHOUSE.

R.M.S. TITANIC.

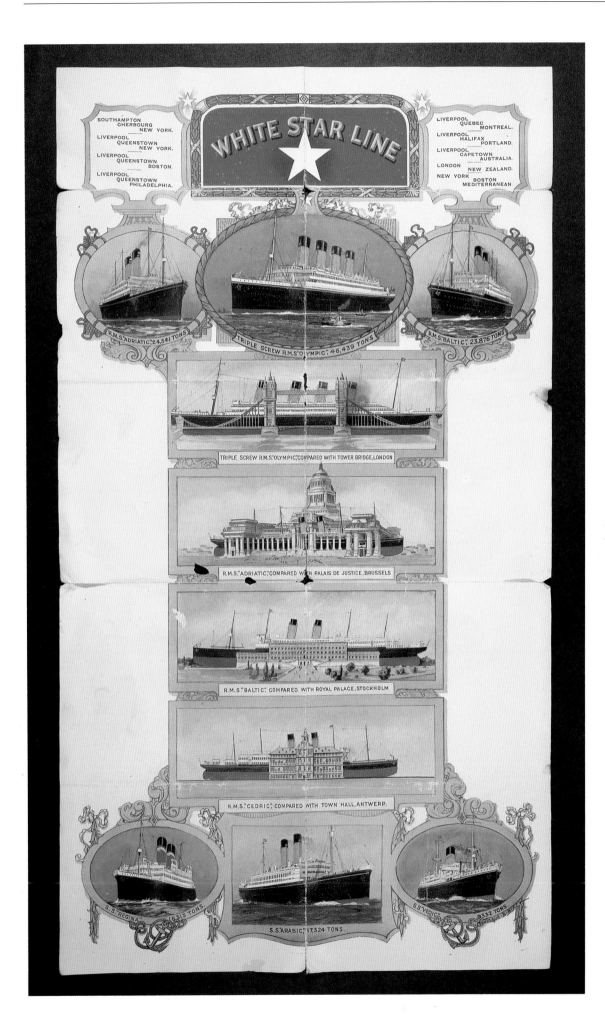

Left: Great ships of the White Star Line. In the early twentieth century Cunard was its only rival. White Star pioneered the concept of luxury at sea.

Left: The Reading and Writing Room of the Titanic, a picture of comfort and elegance.

Right: The *Titanic*, without stacks, being fitted out.

Below: The 'unsinkable' liner with tugs on her maiden voyage.

Above: The sunken bow of the once-great liner with only the fishes for company now.

Ballard later reported at a conference in Washington DC:

Its bow faces north and the ship sits upright on the bottom. Its mighty stacks point upward. . . . It is quiet and peaceful and a fitting place for the remains of this greatest of sea tragedies to rest.

Society mourns the loss of a child because it never had a chance to live out its life. There is a similar note of tremendous regret experienced even today when the *Titanic* is mentioned. She never had a chance to show her worth. It was her maiden voyage. The *Olympic* and the *Britannic*, White Star liners in the same class as *Titanic*, both saw good service.

Although the *Titanic* was built to compete with her Cunard rivals, the emphasis was not so much on swift passage across the Atlantic as on luxury. And no expense was spared. Palm verandas, a Turkish bath, gymnasium, squash court, a hospital with operating room, barber shops, a swimming pool (the first ever on any ship) were just some of the facilities available on board this vast seagoing hotel. A glance at the stocks of tableware taken on board at Southampton shows the kind of service and haute cuisine firstclass passengers could expect: 1000 oyster forks, 1500 crystal dishes, 2000 wine glasses, 1500 champagne glasses, 36,000 oranges, 7000 lettuces, 25,000 lbs of poultry, 75,000 lbs of meat . . . the list goes on.

Left: Comparisons with the heights of various famous monuments revealed the vast size of the *Titanic* and *Olympic*.

Below: Robert Ballard and his team of seafaring adventurers. They brought the *Titanic* back into the public eye.

'Pride comes before a fall' is a sad cliché, but one of the reasons why the *Titanic* has stayed in our memories is related to this saying. She was everything money could buy. She was built by the best builders of her day, Harland and Wolff of Belfast; she was deemed unsinkable; Captain Edward J Smith and his crew were highly experienced. The *Titanic* had everything going for her. So what went wrong? There are many theories and books but ultimately we can only read and study and come to our own conclusions.

The *Titanic* set out on her maiden voyage at approximately noon on 10 April 1912. She was a huge ship and almost came to grief. As she left Southampton *Titanic* displaced so much water that she drew *New York* (American Line) and *Oceanic* (White Star) towards her. Captain Smith's quick thinking, however, prevented a disaster, and the

Titanic docked safely at Cherbourg at seven o'clock that evening, where she picked up more passengers. She stopped again at Cork, in south-west Ireland, and left that town on the 11th. She now carried 1316 passengers and a crew of 891. The dismal Atlantic stretched before her, but the weather was good.

On Sunday 12th the ships *Caronia, Baltic, Amerika, Californian,* and *Mesaba* all reported the movement of icebergs and some of these reports reached the bridge of the *Titanic.* However much we analyze these warnings the fact remains that the *Titanic,* despite her experienced captain and crew, took no special precautions. She steamed ahead at full speed. Speculation as to the reason persists to this day.

On board was a managing director, J Bruce Ismay. Although he was not captain of the ship he had a captain's influence. If at all possible, he wanted the ship to make good time. Captain Smith was due to retire after this voyage. It was a cruel irony that *Titanic*'s maiden voyage was his last. If Ismay had not been on the ship would Captain Smith have been more cautious? *Titanic* steamed ahead at full speed despite the warnings. And Captain Smith did not take an experienced captain's role. This author believes the *Titanic* foundered on the relationship between these two men. A ship, like a dog, serves only one master. Without Ismay, Smith would have been the experienced captain he was. With Ismay he took a chance and thought of retirement.

It was ten o'clock, the sea was calm, there were stars but no moon. The temperature was freezing. Frederick Fleet, on watch, did his duty. He rang three bells and was asked what he saw. His answer goes down in history: 'Iceberg dead ahead!'

Maneuvers were made but a big ship needs time. *Titanic,* unavoidably, struck the iceberg. Many on board thought it was just a little bump, nothing serious.

Titanic stopped. Captain Smith demanded reports of any possible damage. The worst came from Iago Smith, the postal clerk who reported that number one hold was 'filling rapidly.' Then Thomas Andrews, the builder of the ship gave Captain Smith the final news:

CAPTAIN SMITH AND OFFICERS S.S. TITANIC.
Lost on 15th April, 1912, after collision with Iceberg in North Atlantic.
PHOTO BY KENNEDY. 50 YORK ST.

WHAT HAPPENED — THE UNDOING OF THE TITANIC
THE PRECISE NATURE OF THE DAMAGE WROUGHT BY THE ICEBERG

THE BUCKLED PLATES
BILGE KEEL
FIRST CLASS STATE ROOMS
POST MAIL ROOM
DOUBLE BOTTOM
KEEL
ICE PENETRATING THE DOUBLE BOTTOM

Note. The above Section is taken between the Foremast and the First Funnel. For explanation of Bulkheads see page 592.

G. F. MORRELL

The official account of the disaster runs: "Struck berg bluff starboard bow, slight jar, but grinding sound, evidently opening several compartments starboard side." According to a survivor, Mr. Thomas Andrews, one of the Titanic's designers, who lost his life in the catastrophe, went below to investigate the damage, and on his return said, "She is torn to bits below, but will not sink if bulkheads hold. She has been ripped by an underlying peak of ice, and it has torn many of the forward plates from the bolts." The damage caused by the iceberg was all below the water-line.

DRAWN BY G. F. MORRELL

Far left: Captain Smith and Officers of the *Titanic*.

Left: Cross-section showing the damage inflicted by the iceberg.

Below: A rare shot of Captain Smith.

Below left: Some of the rescued being taken aboard the *Carpathia*.

his ship would sink within two hours. Calls for assistance were sent out. The last was: 'The engine is full up to the boilers.'

But Captain Arthur H Rostron of the *Carpathia* was on his way. He pressed his ship as she had never been pressed before. And approximately two hours later he was negotiating ice and picking up survivors. The great ship had gone down with her captain.

Captain Rostron rescued 705 people out of the total of 2200 *Titanic* passengers. He was doubtlessly the hero of the day. But the United States and Great Britain needed a villain. There were several candidates: J Bruce Ismay, a survivor, who 'influenced' the captain to run his ship at full-speed; Captain

Smith himself, too easily swayed perhaps; and Captain Lord of the *Californian*, who failed to respond to reported sightings of rockets when he was much closer to the *Titanic* than the *Carpathia*.

Controversy still rages today as to who was the guilty party. This author's own feeling is that Captain Smith dropped his role as captain at a crucial time.

LUSITANIA

The *Lusitania*, sister ship of the *Mauretania* (Cunard) was a magnificent fast liner. She was 785 feet long, 88 feet broad and rose 200 feet high. She left Pier 54, New York, on 1 May 1915 with 1951 people on board, of which 129 were children. Although there had been warnings in the American press about the threat to shipping from the state of war which existed between Germany and Britain, 159 Americans (neutral at this time) were passengers.

The voyage across the Atlantic went smoothly and Ireland was in sight. But Captain William Turner must have felt some anxiety when he received reports of an active U-boat in the area. At 2.10 pm *Unterseeboote 20* struck the *Lusitania* with deadly torpedoes. An SOS was sent out and ships large and small in the area steamed towards her. But the *Lusitania* was listing so badly that it was difficult to reach the boats on the port side. The deck was covered with people and in the scenario of a horror movie the great ship went down, bows first.

1198 people died including 94 children. Of the 159 Americans on board 124 lost their lives. This disaster united Britain and America in a bond of rage, grief, and condemnation. As the war continued and more American ships were sunk, it became clear to President Woodrow Wilson that he could not tolerate the indiscriminate German war machine. On 6 April 1917 he declared war on Germany. Britain and America were allied in war, allied by the tragedy of the *Lusitania*.

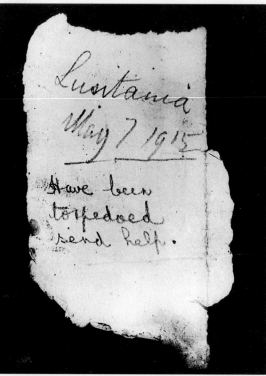

Above: Captain Turner: he stayed on board until the *Lusitania* went down but was later rescued.

Left: A message found in a bottle on a lonely sea shore. Real or fake?

Left: A stark warning and hint of the shape of things to come.

Top: The elegant vision of the *Lusitania* passing the Old Head of Kinsale, Ireland, in 1911.

Above: British soldiers digging three huge graves for victims of the *Lusitania* in Ireland.

ENDURANCE

Sir Ernest Shackleton appropriately named his ship *Endurance*. On a voyage of exploration to the Antarctic she became embedded in ice. The Captain and crew stayed on board the ship from January 1915 to November of the same year. Then the ice crushed her and she sank. Prepared for this eventuality Shackleton and his 27 crew members took to the sea in little boats. They lived in these boats and on ice floes for the duration of the Antarctic summer before making a successful landing on Elephant Island. But his crew were in such poor shape and the conditions so hard that Shackleton knew they had to be rescued. In a 22-foot whaler, *James Caird*, the Captain and five crew covered a perilous 800 miles to a Norwegian whaling station.

There were many dangerous adventures before Shackleton got back to Elephant Island in a small Chilean steamer, *Yelcho*. No-one has ever doubted the courage and in-

tegrity of Shackleton. He rescued his crew and didn't lose a man and the odds he fought against were the toughest the Antartic could offer. Shackleton is rightly seen as an inspiration to all sea-faring explorers.

Above: A truly dramatic shot of Sir Ernest Shackleton's ship *Endurance* caught and crushed in ice.

Left: Sir Ernest Shackleton being presented, ironically, with a bunch of heather for good luck before setting out in the *Endurance*. Despite terrible conditions Shackleton brought all of his crew home alive.

FLYING ENTERPRISE

The whole world loves a hero and Captain Carlsen of an American cargo ship, *Flying Enterprise*, was to have this role thrust on him during the early days of January 1952.

His ship developed cracks in a fierce storm off the north-west point of Spain. Then his rudder went and he was forced to send out an SOS. American and British ships sped to the scene of the listing *Enterprise*. Passengers and crew were rescued but Captain Carlsen remained on board. The tug-boat *Turmoil* which was trying to get a tow on the *Enterprise* was drawn so close to her that ship's mate Kenneth Dancy leapt on to the shattered ship to join Carlsen. The world woke up to heroic actions at sea!

Finally *Turmoil* secured a tow but this was later to break. Carlsen and Dancy were drifting in a sinking ship. On January 8th they were pulled out of the water and the *Flying Enterprise* sank. Captain Carlsen had failed to save his ship but he had done everything a captain could do.

300,000 people lined the streets from Broadway to City Hall in New York to welcome home a modest stubborn captain who had fought so hard not to give up his ship to the merciless sea.

Left: The foundering wreck of the *Flying Enterprise.*

Above: A lifeboat from the *Flying Enterprise* found on rocks off the French coast. Captain Carlsen struggled without success to bring her home to England.

THE MYSTERY OF MISSING SHIPS

THE examples of missing ships or ships found without a crew in this book may be considered 'not modern.' There is then a temptation to say that those mysterious losses happened in the days before radar and radio. Unfortunately even today ships go missing all over the world.

Lloyd's of London, although not the major shipping insurance center it was in the past, records as recently as 1971 that in the period 1961-1971 seventy merchant vessels were posted missing; they went without a trace and more than a thousand lives were lost. The relationship between ship and sea still presents a seemingly unfathomable puzzle.

Two general truths emerge from research into missing ships. First, it is usually smaller vessels which disappear; second, 'ship-jacking' is rare, particularly with ships which are registered because these registered ships carry their credentials on their main beam. They are easily identifiable. There was a case in the early 1900s when the steamer *Ferret* went missing. She left London and failed to arrive at her destination. Where was the *Ferret*? It was quite some time before she was identified in a port in Australia, a rare victim of piracy!

Below: Lloyds of London, the world's most famous society of shipping insurers. The lutine bell, rung in the event of major loss at sea, is visible in the background.

But a cargo ship like the Belgian *Oostmeer* sadly preserves the mystery of the sea. She was new and left Brussels in October 1968. The next day, after she reported her position as close to Algeria, nothing more was heard of her. The *Oostmeer* disappeared. It would not be difficult to list the fate of similar ships.

Because many ships have been lost in an area which has become popularly known as the Bermuda Triangle, theories as to why these ships have disappeared have become fanciful. Crews and ships have been abducted by aliens intent on studying the human life-form. Another suggestion has been that there are monsters or races living beneath the waters who suck our vessels down. When there are no rational answers to a disappea-rance, the human mind is oddly logical: it looks elsewhere and arrives at super-natural forces currently beyond our comprehension. Readers and students and sea-farers must make up their own mind about what is 'out there' . . . storm, fire, explosion, piracy, human error, rocks and reefs . . . or some-thing that is still beyond us.

Strangely enough one of the great events which helped establish the myth of the Bermuda Triangle was not the loss of a ship but the disappearance of five aircraft. In 1945 five US Navy Avengers were lost without a trace. Not a single plane but five! For years the world puzzled. What had happened? Where were the planes? The mystery may, however, soon be solved. In 1991 the Navy Avengers were found. They are under water and may be brought to the surface. We await developments. And naturally we wonder what these planewrecks can tell us about this area of sea.

BERMUDA TRIANGLE

'Bermuda Triangle' is not an official term though I doubt if there exists a captain who does not recognize the name. The Bermuda Triangle refers to part of the Atlantic, from the Caribbean island of Bermuda to southern Florida up to a point past the Antilles, 60°W longitude. In this area many ships and indeed

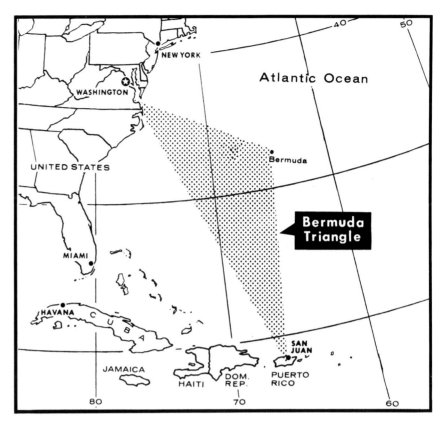

Top: The shaded area of this map indicates the so-called Bermuda Triangle.

Above: A 1974 poster which offers a reward for yet another vessel missing in the Bermuda Triangle.

19

planes have come to grief, disappeared. The sea, the weather here is changeable. There is no doubt about that. Beneath the sea there perhaps lies the ruins of an older civilization. Charles Berlitz, author of *The Bermuda Triangle* and *Atlantis: The Lost Continent Revealed* is an authority on this and I can only recommend that those who feel there is more to this than meets the eye, read his works and make up their own minds.

As for myself, I am convinced there is an old world beneath the waters here but I am not convinced that the buried past has anything to do with the disappearance of ships and aircraft in the area.

SÃO PAULO

After World War II Europe was in great need of metal. Scrap-metal merchants toured the world looking for likely ships which could be towed home and broken up. So it was that the British and Iron Steel Corporation located the old 20,000 ton battleship *São Paulo* in dock at Rio de Janeiro. They bought her and made her sea-worthy. Two powerful tugs, *Dexterous* and *Bustler* were dispatched to bring her back to the United Kingdom.

The towing job went well for more than six weeks. Then in November the three ships were caught in a huge storm off the Azores. The *Dexterous* was damaged and had to slip her tow. Then *Bustler*'s tow broke. At once the captains of the tugs tried to tell the crew of eight on board the *São Paulo* what had happened. There was no reply. The night was dark. This was 1951 and *Bustler* was equipped with up-to-date radar. She tried for soundings. There was nothing. The *São Paulo* had disappeared. The tugs searched for her as later did aircraft of the Royal, Portuguese, and United States' navies. But the *São Paulo* had gone without a trace and it seems that only the unfathomable sea will ever be able to solve the mystery of this sudden dis appearance.

Below: The *Cyclops*, a United States Navy collier, which disappeared without a trace in 1918. She was carrying a cargo of manganese.

USS *CYCLOPS*

On 13 March 1918 the USS *Cyclops* disappeared without a trace and left the world speculating. On board there had been 309 people, passengers, and crew. The US Consul from Rio de Janeiro, two marine lieutenants, 70 enlisted naval men, 15 naval reserve officers, and 221 enlisted personnel made up the ship's company. Not a single body or part of the ship was found.

The *Cyclops* was a sturdy ship. She was built in 1910 and weighed a massive 14,500 tons. She was a collier but at the time of her disappearance was carrying a cargo of manganese from Bahia, Brazil to Norfolk, Virginia. This was war-time and manganese was much needed in the war effort.

The USS *Cyclops* stopped at Georgetown, Guyana and was found to have one engine out of two working. This was not considered to be a real problem; should any trouble arise the *Cyclops* could radio for help. She set off for her destination, Norfolk. Nothing was heard of the ship again. Norfolk reported her over-due and a painstaking search began.

The search involved the American and French navies and merchant vessels in the area. The route of the missing ship was covered; islands, bays and coastlines were thoroughly investigated; radio calls were sent out from all possible points of contact. And all that came out of this was one theory after another. Theories without evidence.

She could have been struck by a floating mine or sunk by a German U-boat. But there was no debris found and it was later ascertained that no German U-boats were operating in the area at that time. She could have been struck by a sudden hurricane but weather reports said there were no hurricanes at that time. Her cargo of manganese could have exploded but again there should have been signs of debris. There was none.

Explanations became more fanciful. There was a time bomb on board! Lieutenant Commander George W Worley, though American, was German-born and he had assisted a U-boat in over-powering the ship's command! She was hi-jacked by enemy agents! All these explanations were far-fetched. The *Cyclops* didn't carry enough fuel

to cross the Atlantic and later when German Admiralty records were captured there was no evidence for saying this ship had been any kind of target.

It is the inexplicable disappearance of ships such as the USS *Cyclops* that has fueled the myth of the 'Bermuda Triangle': there is a force out there, about which we know nothing, and it is taking our ships. Speculation continues to this day.

SS MARINE *SULPHUR* *QUEEN*

The SS Marine *Sulphur Queen* had a crew of 39 and a cargo of molten sulphur brimstone when she left Beaumont, Texas, for her destination of Norfolk, Virginia. The date was 2 February 1963. She was scheduled to deliver her 15,260-ton cargo on 7 February. Thirty-

Below: Father and son display the name-board they found while out walking on a Miami beach. It appeared to be from the bridge of the lost tanker SS Marine *Sulphur Queen*.

Above and below:
Coastguards examine
items from the lost ship,
SS Marine *Sulphur
Queen*. They include
(below) a man's shirt
tied to a lifesaver.

Above right: The missing
tanker, *Sulphur Queen*.

RUBICON

The Cuban ship *Rubicon* was found
abandoned off Key Largo, Florida, on 22
October 1944. Her life-boats were missing
and there were signs that the crew had left in
a hurry. There was a survivor on board but he
could not speak. The survivor was a dog, half-
dead with starvation. What a tale he might
have told! And why had he been left behind?

All these ships fall approximately into an
area known as the Bermuda Triangle.

Ivan Sanderson, an American sea-observer,
has some unusual theories. He has noted that
it is unusual for a crew to abandon ship and
not take their pets with them. He goes further
than this and says that super-human 'entities'
are responsible for kidnapping whole crews so
that their progress may be studied. He draws
attention to abandoning cats, dogs and
canaries while parrots disappear with the
human crew. The reason for this is that the
'aliens' know that the gift of speech indicates
the dominant race on earth. Is an alien
studying the limited speech of a parrot a little
too far-fetched? Ivan Sanderson, logically,
would say that it isn't.

five hours after departure Captain James V
Fanning reported his ship's position as being
200 miles off Key West in the straits of
Florida. So far so good. But that was the last
that was heard from the big tanker and she
was presumed lost on 4 February.

What happened to her? Coast Guard vessels from Virginia, Northern California,
Florida and Louisiana began the hunt, but
without success. Then a navy patrol boat
located white sticks of wood and a yellow
substance in the water, east of Florida. The

Coast Guard patrol boat *Sweet Gum* investigated but reported that, although the *Sulphur
Queen* had a white super-structure, this
debris was not part of her remains. There fol-
lowed another week of searching but nothing
more was found. The search was called off.

Then round about 20 February various
ships began to find things which were from
the *Sulphur Queen*: a life jacket, seven life pre-
servers (one used), four life rings (sadly, one
with a man's shirt attached), and some pieces
of the ship's name board. The Coast Guard
concluded that two crewmen had survived
but then probably met their death by drowning or sharks.

As with the disappearance of the USS
Cyclops explanations and theories were rife.
The *Sulphur Queen* had leaked sulphur gas
and exploded. She'd struck a floating mine.
She'd been sabotaged. The Cubans had taken

her. She had broken in half and sunk.

As fast as the theories came up they were knocked down. Escape vents would mostly take care of leaking gas and an explosion would have been minimal. A great tanker takes time to sink so there should have been time for radio contact. Cuban involvement was considered, finally, to be too fanciful.

No bodies, life-boats, oil slick, or floating sulphur were found and no mayday was sent out. The *Sulphur Queen* had disappeared and served to feed rumors about that area of water known as the Bermuda Triangle.

CAROL DEERING

The *Carol Deering* beached on a North Carolina shore in February 1921. The ship was boarded and it was found that dinner was about to be served. Obviously the crew had made a hasty departure, but why? Surely the food couldn't have been that bad. The disappearance of the crew remains a mystery to this day.

JOHN AND MARY

In April 1932 the *John and Mary* was found deserted 50 miles due south of Bermuda. There was no sign of the crew and no clues to their disappearance.

Above: Later it was revealed a fortunate six were rescued!

GLORIA COLITE

When the *Gloria Colite* was reported adrift in the Bay of Mexico on 3 February 1940, she was a ghost ship. On board there was no sign of her crew of nine.

The US Coast Guard cutter *Cardigan* went out to investigate what had happened to the 125 foot schooner. Her position was approximately 150 miles due south of Mobile, Alabama.

The *Cardigan* took the *Gloria Colite* in tow and radioed back strange details: the decks were wrecked, her foresails were badly torn, the mainsail, the rigging, and the steering wheel had gone . . . and of course there was nobody to tell the tale of what had happened.

On the afternoon of the 5th the Cardigan reached Mobile with her mysterious ship in tow.

The *Gloria Colite* was examined carefully for an explanation. An investigation revealed nothing.

Once again voices murmured about the Bermuda Triangle and the sea kept its secrets.

MARY CELESTE

The *Mary Celeste* was a derelict found under such mysterious circumstances that Captain David Morehouse of the *Dei Gratia* who discovered the abandoned ship was later to be tried for murder and conspiracy. His presumed motive was the reward of salvage; apart from the ship itself there were 1701 barrels of alcohol valued at $42,000 on board.

Where were the ship's crew of ten, the captain's wife, his baby daughter, and the ship's cat? There was no sign of them. Other facts deepened the mystery: hatch doors open, no boats, a broken compass, no sign of the sextant or ship's papers, valuable personal articles left behind, no distress signals displayed, the galley was ship-shape and the dinner table clean.

The British brigantine *Dei Gratia* was between the Azores and Portugal when she found the brigantine *Mary Celeste* on 4 December 1872. Evidence pointed toward a hasty departure: the Captain had left his rain coat and a sailor his pipe. Speculation raged.

Below: The story of the *Mary Celeste* has contributed greatly to the myth or reality of the Bermuda Triangle. She's seen here in full sail, under her original name, the *Amazon*.

Captain Morehouse brought the *Mary Celeste* to Gibraltar, a journey of some six hundred miles, no mean feat, but if he won his salvage claim it would certainly have been worth it. Things did not quite turn out as he would have liked. Although he was cleared of murder charges he was only awarded the sum of 8300 dollars.

The mystery of the *Mary Celeste* was never solved but she was made sea-worthy and sailed the seas until Captain Gilman Parker of Winthrop, Massachusetts, destroyed her on a coral reef in the West Indies with the goal of obtaining insurance money. But he was out of luck and his plot discovered! So ended the *Mary Celeste* but not her mysterious story which is still with us today.

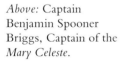

Above: Captain Benjamin Spooner Briggs, Captain of the *Mary Celeste*.

Above right: The Captain's wife and their son Arthur Stanley Briggs both disappeared along with the rest of the ship's complement.

Right: The *Dei Gratia* the ship which came across the empty, drifting *Mary Celeste*; from a painting by Giuseppe Coli, 1873.

COLLISION!

THESE days large ships carry Automatic Radar Plotting Aids which enable them to receive not only an accurate picture of the movements of other ships but also what their speed is. Thus the modern vessel has become 'wary' of its neighbors. The most sophisticated radar equipment will even automatically sound the alarm if the ship is on a collision course.

For a happy moment then it looks as though collision at sea will be a thing of the past by the end of the century. But of course this isn't the case for several reasons. Human negligence and mechanical failure can never truly be expunged. The waterways of the world are becoming increasingly busy. A modern ship is so huge and heavy that a captain must act in good time if he is to avoid a collision.

Progress in safety at sea continues but not without some disasters.

MARCHIONESS/ BOWBELLE

On 20 August 1989 the dredger *Bowbelle* smashed into the pleasure boat *Marchioness* and sank her. Fifty-one people drowned in the River Thames, London. The youngest victim was Francesca Dallaglio, a talented ballerina who had danced before the Princess of Wales. The girl's mother said of the rescue operation:

A number of victims were swimming in the water for between twenty and forty minutes while the main rescue boats went past them 'en route' for Battersea Bridge.

Right: The London Fire Brigade scans the River Thames for survivors from the *Marchioness.*

Below right: The beached wreck of the *Marchioness.*

Below: The ferry *Dona Paz* which sank off the central Philippines with 1500 people on board. She had collided with an oil tanker.

Above: A police launch with its sad cargo of body bags from the *Marchioness*.

Is it significant that the *Bowbelle* has been involved in nine collisions since 1965?

The survivors and relatives of the victims are rightly pressing for a public inquiry and many feel there has been a cover-up. We have certainly not heard the last of this case in 1991.

QUEEN MARY, HMS CURACOA

During World War II the 80,000-ton Cunard liner *Queen Mary* was adapted to become a troop-carrying ship from the United States to the United Kingdom. The liner was so huge that she could carry as many as 10,000 men. She crossed the Atlantic alone but on reaching Northern Ireland picked up an escort. This was on account of the German U-boat activity in the area. On 2 October 1942 Queen Mary's escort was the 4200-ton cruiser *HMS Curacoa*, along with a number of destroyers.

Captain Henderson of the *Bowbelle* was charged with 'failing to keep a proper lookout.' He denied these charges. The prosecution also stated that the communication system between the bridge and the bow was faulty. For two days a jury deliberated on the tragic events but were unable to reach a verdict. They were then discharged by the judge.

Many questions remain currently unanswered. Can the Thames cope with a ship the size of the *Bowbelle*? Was there sufficient crew on each boat to deal with an emergency? How efficient is the Port of London Authority in dealing with rescue operations?

The liner sailed a zig-zag course so as not to make herself an easy torpedo target. *Curacoa* was apparently aware of the zig-zag course but, incredible as it may seem, things went drastically and tragically wrong. The ships approached one another and there was nearly a collision. Maneuvering grew complicated. Then there was a collision. The mighty liner went right through the smaller ship and cut her in two. *Queen Mary* was holed but did not sink. *Curacoa* sank with 300 men on board.

Right: The buckled stairway of the liner *Queen Mary* after a rough Atlantic crossing.

Left: Tugs pulling the stranded *Queen Mary* out of Cherbourg harbor.

Captain Illingworth did not stop his ship to pick up possible survivors. He signalled to HMS *Bulldog* what had happened. He dared not risk the 10,000 American servicemen he had on board. Captain Coutwood, skipper of the Curacoa survived.

For years the courts wrangled as to who was at fault before apportioning blame: two thirds to *Curacoa*, one third to *Queen Mary*.

ANDREA DORIA

The *Andrea Doria* was the pride of the Italian luxury class of liner. She had made a successful voyage from Genoa and was two hundred miles from her destination, New York, when a dense fog descended. Captain Piero Calamai sounded his foghorn. All was as it should be.

Five miles away the Swedish liner *Stockholm* under the command of Captain Gunnar Nordenson was outward bound. Some passengers were later to report they saw the *Stockholm* coming and knew a collision was imminent and unavoidable.

Death came quickly for people on both ships as the *Stockholm* ripped a 40-foot hole in the starboard side of the *Andrea Doria*. The two ships exchanged frantic messages. The

Italian liner was listing badly and water was pouring in. She carried 1134 passengers and 575 crew. On board the *Stockholm* there were 750. But the *Stockholm*, although she suffered casualties, some of them fatal, was not sinking. Her bow had been smashed as though by a gigantic fist.

As is often the case with badly listing ships *Andrea Doria* was unable to launch her life boats. An SOS went out and reached the coastguard. Ships were dispatched immediately.

The *Ile de France*, a French ship under the command of Captain Raoul de Beaudean, picked up the SOS and steamed toward the scene of the collision. Fortune favored the brave. The fog lifted. *Ile de France* hove into view of the *Andrea Doria* with her life-boats at the ready. A cheer went up.

In all Captain de Beaudean picked approximately 1700 survivors from the stricken liner.

Above left: A sailor admires the 30,000-ton flagship *Andrea Doria*.

Above: The *Andrea Doria* goes down in a turmoil of debris.

Left: Officials inspect the bows of the *Stockholm* opened like a tin.

Far left: The Italian liner off Nantucket shortly before she sank.

He carried them to New York at full steam. A total of fifty people lost their lives.

But as so often with disaster at sea a mystery remained. How had the collision happened at all? The sinking of the *Andrea Doria* happened in 1956 and both liners were equipped with the latest radar. The puzzle has never satisfactorily been solved.

ALVA CAPE

Explosion, so often the cause of ships' disasters, occurred when the *Alva Cape*, a British tanker, struck the American tanker SS *Texaco Massachusetts* in New York harbor on 19 June 1966. The British ship burst into flames and sank. She was carrying a cargo of naphtha, an inflammable oil distilled from coal. Some lives were lost but the disaster did not end here.

On 28 June while salvaging operations were underway, a series of explosions rocked the wreck and killed four more people and injured seven.

The US Coast Guard criticized the way salvage was handled and said there should have been a marine chemist supervising procedures when such a delicate and volatile cargo was involved.

Below: The *Alva Cape* and the *Texaco Massachusetts* on fire. Tugs fought to keep them away from oil tanks in New Jersey, seen in the background of this photograph.

Above: A fireboat struggles to dowse the flames threatening to engulf the British tanker *Alva Cape*.

Left: The *Alva Cape* is towed out of New York harbor to be scuttled. She carried 10,000 barrels of deadly naphtha.

FIRE DOWN BELOW

IF there is a hell on earth, fire at sea must come close to it. It is not just a ship which is on fire, it is often the water around the ship. Thus a leap into the sea or the launching of a boat can be as deadly as staying on board. I include here two quotations from very fortunate survivors of fire at sea.

The SS *City of Guildford* was ablaze in the Mediterranean. The ship's purser, Mr E R Robison gave some timely advice:

I told them to take off their life-jackets to enable them to swim faster through the flames . . . I came across two soldiers, so pulling off their life-jackets I just pushed them overboard. Both these men managed to swim clear of the flames and were rescued . . . The flames spread over the after part of the ship and the surrounding waters. There was no alternative, other than dive through the blazing water, so I dived from the poop, the impetus carrying me a considerable distance under water. I continued swimming under water until I thought my lungs would burst but on coming to the surface I realised that the effort had been worthwhile, as I was just on the outside of the blazing water, about seventy feet away from the ship.

The SS *Portsea* blew up in the Mediterranean and nearly took Able Seaman H W T

Below: An aerial photo of the French liner *L'Atlantique* on fire in the English Channel.

Above: Dense smoke covers the ferry, *Scandanavian Star.* More than a hundred people lost their lives in this horrific accident.

Right: Fire-fighters are lowered on to the *Scandinavian Star*'s deck.

Left: The *Morro Castle* wrecked and beached at Asbury Park, 10 September 1934.

Below: Coast Guard RW Hodge was the first to board the stricken vessel.

Woods with it. But he was destined to be one of the lucky ones:

I was blown high into the air . . . I regained consciousness and found myself swimming under water. I continued to swim until I came to the surface, only to find myself in the middle of a mass of burning oil with nothing to be seen of the ship but her two masts which were sticking up out of the water. I dived under the water again, and although I am not a good swimmer, managed to keep going until I saw that I was clear of the burning oil which appeared as a dark shadow above me.

In war-time the incidence of fires at sea naturally increases. To give a feeling of what it looked like and the ferocity and power of fire I quote from Captain R D Macfarlane's account of sailing through it whilst on convoy duty in the Mediterranean in World War II:

The sea was one sheet of fire and as we were so close we had to steam through it. I put the helm hard-a-port and had to come down from where I was on monkey island to the bridge to save myself from being burned. It seemed as if we had been enveloped in flame and smoke for years, although it was only a matter of minutes, otherwise the ship could never have survived. The flames were leaping mast high – indeed, air pilots reported that at times they reached 2000 feet. The heat was terrific. The air was becoming drier every minute, as though the oxygen was being sucked out of it, as in fact it was. When we inspected the damage afterwards we found that nearly all the paint on the ship's sides had been burnt away and the bottoms of the lifeboats reduced to charcoal.

Hell on earth, indeed, but for those who have survived fire at sea the world must have looked like heaven.

MORRO CASTLE

The story of the luxurious passenger ship *Morro Castle* is mysterious, horrific, and chaotic. On 7 September 1934 she was returning from Havana to New York and due to dock at her pier in the early hours of the morning. That evening, however, her Captain, Robert Wilmott, had been found dead in his bath. A heart attack was suspected. First Mate William Warms anxiously took command.

It was about 2.30 am when a few late-night drinkers noticed a locker on fire. They fought the blaze while the ship's bosun was down below, drunk. The ship was soon a mass of flame but it was not until about an hour later that the acting Captain sent out an SOS call. Chaos reigned. The fire equipment didn't work. Wind fanned the flames. Gunpowder exploded. Half-empty life-boats didn't stop to pick up drowning passengers.

The fishing community of New Jersey played a sterling part in the rescue of the living and the dead. Finally a Coast Guard ship took the *Morro Castle* on tow but then the tow broke and she was beached at Ash-

Above: The sad remains of passengers' clothing.

Below: Some of the fortunate who escaped the inferno.

37

bury Park, New Jersey, still belching clouds of black smoke. Of the 548 passengers and crew 134 lost their lives.

The unlikely hero of the day was Chief Radio Operator Rogers, who stayed at his post under dangerous conditions. He survived to tell the tale and was duly feted. Later, however, Rogers's life of crime came to light and he died in prison as a murderer.

SS NORONIC

Another harbor disaster though not with the shore consequences of Grandcamp occurred when the SS *Noronic* caught fire in Toronto harbor. The ship was a Canadian pleasure cruiser, 362 feet long and five decks high. She carried 524 passengers and a crew of 171.

At 1.30 in the morning most of the passengers were on board when the fire was discovered. Within minutes 18 fire-engines arrived but they were too late. The ship was well ablaze and there was pandemonium. Men and women were trapped. Others fought each other to get off the roaring death-trap. Some jumped safely to the pier. Others

were fished out of the water. They were the lucky ones. In all, 120 people perished and firemen were later to talk of charred, embracing skeletons. The tragedy at that time was described as the worst on the Great Lakes in more than a hundred years. Criticism was levelled at Captain Taylor for having only 15 crewmen on board at the time of the fire and his master's licence was temporarily suspended.

Above: The *Noronic*, cruise ship of the Great Lakes, in a sea of flames, 18 September 1949.

Right: An aerial photo of the *Noronic* burning in her Toronto dock. Most of the victims were Americans from the Mid-West.

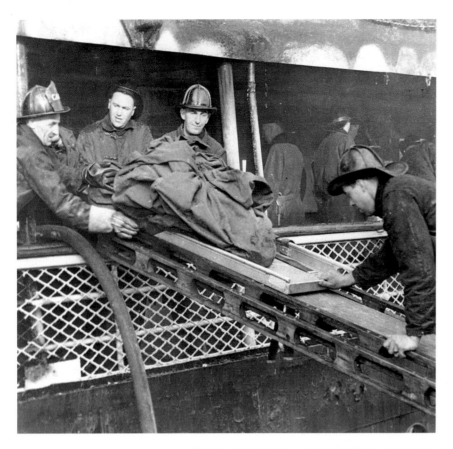

Above: In an effort to beat each other with the most gruesome reports, some New York newspapers' greatly exaggerated the numbers of dead.

Left: Firemen faced with the gruesome job of removing the victims from the gutted ship.

Below: The make-shift mortuary in a Toronto horticultural building.

Right: The French freighter *Grandcamp* in her heyday.

GRANDCAMP

Fire in a harbor can be as disastrous as fire at sea, as the people of Texas City, Texas were to discover on that blackest of days for the community: 16 April 1947. A French freighter, the *Grandcamp*, was moored on the water-front there with a cargo of ammonium nitrate. The ship caught fire. Attempts to extinguish the fire and tow the *Grandcamp* out to sea failed. Within half an hour she blew up. Worse was to follow. The ship's explosion had a domino effect. The Monsanto Chemical Company exploded and then the Stone Oil Refinery. And hours later the SS *High Flyer*, also with a cargo of ammonium nitrate, exploded.

Hundreds of people died. At the Monsanto plant alone 227 people lost their lives. Fifty acres of the area was destroyed. Nothing was left of the *Grandcamp*. This fire which started on a ship was a tragedy for the people on land, the community of Texas City, Texas.

Left: The luxury French liner *Normandie* in a pall of smoke after she caught fire on the Hudson River.

Right: All that remained of the grand staircase of the USS *Lafayette,* formerly called the *Normandie.*

Above: This wartime photograph of the *Normandie* has been lightly censored, presumably to conceal troopship conversion work.

NORMANDIE

Desperately short of ships after the attack on Pearl Harbor, France leant her huge luxury liner (79,280 tons and 1029 feet long) the *Normandie* to the United States.

The *Normandie* was at pier 88 in New York City undergoing conversion work so that she could function as a troopship for the United States Navy when a spark from a blowtorch set a pile of life-vest, on fire. The fire quickly spread and thousands of gallons of water were pumped into the ship, so much water in fact that the great liner sank. This was a great blow for the US Navy who had to compensate France for the loss.

The *Normandie* sank on 9 February 1942 and ended up in the scrapyard.

DAVY JONES'S LOCKER

Below: The Captain of a capsized yacht clings to his mast – and his life.

Right: Sir Francis Chichester's yacht *Gipsy Moth IV* rounds Cape Horn in a gale.

ALL you can expect from the sea and the weather is the unexpected. It is no wonder that sailors the world over are superstitious. There was even a man who deserted the *Titanic* in Ireland before it sailed on to disaster. Afterwards he said he had left because he had a funny feeling about the ship.

The unexpected finding and rescue of men at sea must be a strange and uplifting experience. Survivors of course must always expect to be rescued. When that hope dies life will too.

The American Liberty ship *Compass* was certainly not combing the sea for missing ships or persons when she was near the Azores (where the *São Paulo* disappeared) in 1952. Suddenly she saw a flotilla of tiny yellow open boats pitching and heaving on an angry Atlantic.

The men were in a terrible condition. They had been at sea for a week in open-boats 14 feet long, in huge gales. They had eaten nothing and survived physically by sucking water from their rain-soaked caps. These fishermen who escaped the sinking of their

Above: Sir Francis Chichester and *Gipsy Moth IV* at full stretch in open sea.

mother ship, the Portuguese *João Costa*, in their dories, as they are known, were as used to these little boats as the Vikings to their long-ships. They fished from them and being used to them were not sea-sick. Under such conditions sea-sickness can be fatal as it drains the body's fluids. So there was an element of experience in their lucky rescue.

SAILING

If a citizen of the United States or the United Kingdom went through the magazine section of a newsagent, they might be surprised to see the large number of periodicals on yachting. Motor power may have replaced sailing power at a commercial and transport level but sails are here to stay for leisure and competition. Yachting folk range from the 'messing-about-in-boats' type to the fiercely competitive; and then there are the solitary figures who circumnavigate the globe or cross the Atlantic.

The Fastnet Race attracts an international gathering. But there are many other races. In San Diego in 1992 trials begin for the challenger section of the America's Cup. This is a prestige race and Britain is currently scraping around to find sponsorship for an American Cup-class yacht.

Competition aside, people who like to sail explain their loving obsession in terms of freedom, peace, and danger. They feel stripped to the basis and alone with (or against) nature.

The best quotations come from those sailors who have pressed themselves to the limits. Sir Francis Chichester in *Gipsy Moth IV* said of an experience in the Tasman Sea:

The boat had heeled over to at least 41 degrees below the horizontal before it righted itself. It must have been a fantastic wave. I was frightened. I thought that if this can happen in an ordinary storm, what would it be like if I ran into a real hurricane . . .? The capsize left me in low spirits.

Dr David Lewis said of his crossing of the

north Atlantic in 1960 in *Cardinal Vertue*:

When I was very tired, and had spent monotonous hours at the helm in winds too light for the vane, I sometimes heard voices . . . Hallucinations seemed to occur only when solitude and fatigue are accompanied by monotonous occupations . . . I would think that varying tasks demanding physical and/or mental effort would be valuable in preserving emotional stability.

Plainly life alone at sea will tax the individual to the extreme. There is identification with the body and the vessel and the mind and the wayward elements of nature.

Joshua Slocum in his sailing yacht *Spray*,

alone in the north Atlantic, found himself pushed into the realms of fantasy:

I realized that the sloop was plunging into a heavy sea, and, looking out of the companionway, to my amazement I saw a tall man at the helm. One may imagine my astonishment. His rig was that of a foreign sailor.

The sailor, pilot of Columbus's ship, spoke to Captain Slocum:

I am the pilot of *Pinta* come to aid you. Lie quiet, Señor Captain, you have calentura, but you will be all right tomorrow.

Calentura is said to be a sailors' disease in

Above: Ted Turner at the helm of *Tenacious*, winner of the Fastnet race in 1979, the year disaster struck.

45

Top: Tenacious with the
wind in her sails.

Above: The *Ariadne,*
which lost four of her
six crew, in happier
times.

which they imagine the sea to be a green field
and are then filled with a desire to jump into
it. Captain Slocum's vision, be it real or a
mental projection, was a warning for him.

The weekend sailors on the local stretch of
river or coast-line need not worry about this.
But it is interesting to note that the further
afield a sailor pushes himself or herself in
their yacht, the further they will push themselves mentally, physically, and emotionally.
Yachting people at all stages know this. The
sea is out there. With a sail and the wind it is
always a challenge of some kind. Human
beings feel the need for challenge and sail.
Both big and little sailors have their stories to
tell.

FASTNET

The Fastnet Race for sailing yachts has an
international following and in 1979 was won
by an American, Ted Turner, in his 61 foot-
yacht *Tenacious*. The newspapers were not to
carry pictures of the winner that year but of
the devastation that occurred at sea.

1979 saw the biggest entry in the event,
with 303 yachts of varying sizes and classes.
The race begins at the Isle of Wight, passes
the Fastnet Rock (south coast of Ireland) and
finishes in Plymouth, south-west England.

On Saturday 11 August the weather was
fine and the boats set off, a glorious sight. By
the 14th the picture had changed dramatically. The boats were scattered over an area
of 20,000 square miles. Huge gales had
blown in from North America. The first distress calls were sent out. Rescue operations
which were to last four days began. Irish and
English life-boats went out. The Royal Navy
and Air Force were called in. Wessex helicopters pulled many a weary sailor from a
smashed boat in a pitching sea. Without the
helicopters many more lives would have
been lost. Of the tragic tales later to be told
perhaps an American yacht, *Ariadne*, had the
saddest. She lost four of her six crew.

A Total of 15 people died. 194 boats gave
up the race, five sank and 19 were abandoned.
85 yachts actually finished the race but there
was nothing to celebrate unless it was survival in the teeth of a storm.

HERALD OF FREE ENTERPRISE

Fresh in the minds of many people in the United Kingdom is the unexpected capsizing of the car ferry, the *Herald of Free Enterprise*. This shocking disaster occurred in the little Belgian harbor of Zeebrugge on 6 March 1987.

The *Herald* was just moving out of harbor when the Belgian Coastguard received word that she was listing. The time was 18.46. At 18.47 she capsized on to her port side, destroying her life-boats. Many people were drowned instantly in the freezing water. Others were able to climb up on to the starboard side and wait for rescue. Within fifteen minutes, warships, helicopters and small vessels were combing the waters and lifting survivors to safety. Later, divers were confronted with the macabre task of bringing out bodies trapped below. 188 people died.

Top: The *Herald Of Free Enterprise* with rescue workers on board.

Above: Salvage work begins on the British ferry at Zeebrugge, Belgium.

The enquiry into the tragedy was long and painstaking. But a conclusion was finally reached. No-one was directly responsible for seeing that the bow doors of the ferry were closed and it was through these doors that the water poured. The company, Townsend Thoresen, took full responsibility for what had happened and future procedures were changed: the captain was always to be informed that the doors were shut before leaving harbor. This revision of procedures of course came too late for the many grieving families.

Left: Giant cranes pull the *Herald Of Free Enterprise* upright in Zeebrugge Harbor.

Above: The *Royal George* off Deptford Harbor, from a painting by John Clevely.

ROYAL GEORGE

In 1782 the Royal Navy ship *Royal George* was the second largest ship in the fleet. She was at anchor off Spithead, England, taking on stores and making ready for the Mediterranean. She was a hive of activity with men, women, children, and animals on board. The sea was flat and the day sunny. A small vessel, the *Lark*, was attached to her port side unloading barrels of rum. Suddenly the ship's carpenter noticed she was taking on water through the gun holes. Before the ship could be bailed out or abandoned she went over, trapping and drowning in the region of a thousand souls. For days after this tragedy clusters of bodies broke the surface.

The *Royal George* remained in 65 feet of water for nearly sixty years before she was blown up in the first operation of its kind.

STEAM AND PADDLE POWER

Above: The smashed hull of the steamship *Columbia*.

WITH its high decks and ungainly wheel the paddle-steamer is an awkward-looking vessel. But like so many designs, with the passing of time it has gained in beauty and probably romance.

The paddle-wheel has been with us for hundreds of years: the Romans had oxen on board to turn theirs! The wheel drives a vessel through the water by paddles which radiate from a shaft similar to that of a coach wheel.

Steam was introduced in the late 1700s. There was a French steamer in operation in 1783 and in the United States John Fitch ran a steam vessel service in 1790 on the Delaware River. By the early nineteenth century 'side-wheelers' and 'stern-wheelers' could be seen chugging up and down the Mississippi.

The first American steamship on a regular route across the Atlantic was the 1700-ton, *Washington*. She made her maiden voyage in 1847. In 1850 the Collins Line won the Blue Ribband which was the legendary symbol of the fastest crossing of the Atlantic. Steam power was, however, used as an auxiliary to sail power: a vessel at this time had both.

Perhaps the most famous steamship was the *Great Eastern*. She was a side-wheeler and made her first voyage in 1860. She was made of iron and was the biggest steamship built for half a century. She had five smokestacks and six masts.

Despite her screw propeller, which succeeded paddle wheels on ocean-going ships, the *Great Eastern* could not really pay her way. But she left her mark in history: between 1865 and 1866 she laid the first Atlantic cable, and the United States of America and the United Kingdom drew a little closer to each other.

GENERAL SLOCUM

There is a monument in the Lutheran Cemetary, Queens, New York to 958 victims of the steamboat *General Slocum* which caught fire on the Hudson River on 15 June 1904. A

Above: A photo of the sinking steamer, *Cobequid*. Boats are seen rescuing passengers and mail.

worse tragedy is hard to imagine. In all 1031 people were declared missing or dead and most of these were women and children.

The *General Slocum* was packed to the rails with Sunday-school classes when a fire broke out near Hell Gate, New York City. A breeze fanned the blazing woodwork and turned the steamer into a burning hell. Many of those who went overboard were caught and killed in the paddle wheels. Others drowned.

Right: The burned-out frame of the *General Slocum*.

Above: The sad and grisly task of pulling victims of the *General Slocum* tragedy from the water.

If any good can be said to come out of such horror it was to be found in the enforcement of new safety regulations. President Theodore Roosevelt was justifiably angry and personally fired a number of marine inspectors. The standard of steamers was gradually improved over a number of years.

As for the wreck of the *General Slocum*, it was raised and became a coal barge, *Maryland*. The *Maryland* found her final resting place at the bottom of the sea off New Jersey in 1912.

Right: Victims of the *General Slocum* laid out by the river.

CITY OF COLUMBUS

Captain Wright of the steamer *City of Columbus* was rightly deemed to be at fault when he ran his ship on to hidden rocks off Martha's Vineyard island on 17 January 1884.

He was bound for Savannah, Georgia, with a crew of 45 and 87 passengers when he made his fatal error. He tried to back his ship off the rocks but only succeeded in holing her. Icy water poured in and many died in their bunks. Others climbed up to the rigging where they were to perish in the freezing weather. Only 29 people survived this ordeal and the captain was one of them. A court of inquiry rescinded his ship's licence.

EASTLAND

The *Eastland* was one of five pleasure steamers berthed in the Chicago River. She had three decks, was 265 feet long, and was one of the swiftest ships operating in the Lakes area. Her reputation was not good despite twelve years of service. This rumor didn't bother the crowd assembled on the morning of 24 July

Above: The *City of Columbus* disappears beneath the waves. More than a hundred people died because of a captain's error.

Below: The *Eastland* lies on its side in dock on the Chicago River. Hundreds were drowned when it keeled over.

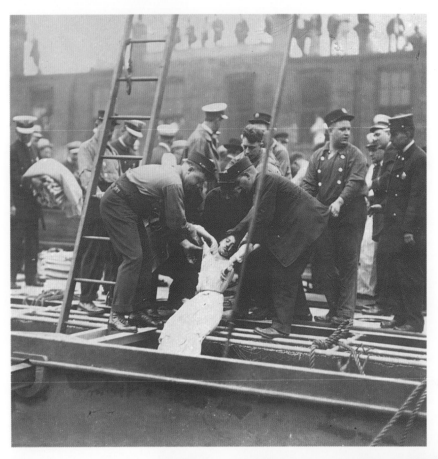

1915. They were only concerned with their trip. They scrambled aboard.

From the start things were not right. The ship, with the weight of the passengers, listed to starboard. Captain Pedersen adjusted his ship by partly filling his port tanks. Then she listed to port. She was at this time secured by hawser to the tug *Kenosha*. Then suddenly a terrible thing happened. The *Eastland* rolled over and threw hundreds of men, women and children into the water. Panic set in.

The *Eastland* had a capacity for about 2500 people and it was generally thought she had about that number on board when the tragedy happened. Although close to shore, 812 people drowned. Without the *Kenosha* the figure would have been much higher. The tug became in fact a bridge to shore for the lucky survivors.

The individual history of a ship is often strange. After this terrible disaster, *Eastland* wasn't scrapped. She was repaired and became the USS *Wilmette*. As such, she wasn't scrapped until 1946.

Above: A dead woman in a white dress is pulled from the wreck of the *Eastland*.

Right: Identifying the serried ranks of *Eastland* victims.

Left: Seven coffins for seven who died from one family.

Below: This photo strikes a happier note as survivors of the *Eastland* tragedy trail across the bridge the *Kenosha* provides.

MAINE

The steamer *Maine* met a sorry end with ice
and flames. On 4 February 1920 she was on
her way from New York to Bridgeport,
Connecticut, when she became embedded in
thick ice in Long Island sound. The tide
turned but only drove the steamer on to a
shelf of rocks near Execution Rocks. She was
holed and water poured into the lower decks.

Things could have turned out worse
although the crew and passengers underwent
a gruelling three days before they were
rescued by a freight lighter, who also rescued
the horses on board.

The New England Steamship Company
considered a salvage operation too costly and
took anything of value from the steamer and
left her. Later, because her wooden structure
could prove a danger to a nearby lighthouse,
she was torched and went up in a huge con-
flagration of smoke and flame. Only the re-
maining steel parts were salvaged. A sorry
end for a beautiful steamer.

CEPHEUS

The *Cepheus*, a steamer owned by the Iron
Steamboat Company, had a good captain on
board. On 12 August 1892 she struck a hidden
object and was badly holed. The captain,
however, managed to run her into shallow
water at Norton Point. His ship of 578 tons
was later raised and towed into Brooklyn
docks.

GATE CITY

Thick fog was the undoing of the steamer
Gate City. This steamer of the Savannah Line
came to grief when she lost her bearings and
beached at Moriches, Long Island, New
York. 48 people were saved from the *Gate
City* and some of her cargo was saved too.
The ship itself was beyond salvage, a com-
plete wreck.

EMMELINE

The steamer *Emmeline* had a nasty accident on
11 July 1900. She was on the Hudson River,

New York, when she struck the Newburgh dock. Nothing could be done and the steamer sank. But she was not lost for ever. The *Emmeline* was later raised, refitted and lived to sail again.

JOHN H STARIN

The weight of the freight steamer *John H Starin* was the cause of her wrecking on the night of 19 February 1909.

She was built in 1865 to carry revenue as a cutter and was later refitted. On the night of her loss she was heavily weighed down with cargo and fighting a terrible gale off Long Island Sound, the scene of many a wreck. Her seams began to open and all hands were summoned to man the pumps, but to little avail. Water continued to pour in and rose up the bodies of the working crew.

Then the pilot located the lights of the breakwater at Steeplechase Island. With renewed vigor the crew pumped for all they were worth. Then the steamer lost the lights and foundered on rocks. The crew and part of the cargo were saved but *John H Starin* was a write-off and would never take to the sea again.

NORUMBEGA

On 13 August 1912 the steamboat *Norumbega* suffered a dramatic and totally unexpected grounding at Clarks Point just by Northeast Harbor. Although there was thick fog her trip was only across the harbor. The firemen stoked her up ready for the crossing. For some reason there was a short wait before she set off. The result was that the vessel lost power mid-way to her destination and ploughed aground. She listed dangerously but was hauled afloat. Inspection revealed that the *Norumbega* had suffered little damage and she sailed again but with less drama.

IROQUOIS

The steamer *Iroquois*, previously named the *Kennebec*, came aground on 27 March 1913 in the Hudson River. A dark night and thick fog were the causes of the accident. Attempts by the *C W Morse* to haul the *Iroquois* afloat failed when the tow-line snapped. The *Iroquois* was stranded for seven days on a bank before *Champion*, a wrecking steamer, managed to pull her off.

Left: The *Emmeline* docks in a rather unorthodox and unsatisfactory manner.

Below left: The career of the *Norumbega* suffers a dramatic set-back.

Bottom left: The *Iroquois* towers above local housing after grounding in the Hudson River.

Below: Little remains to salvage from the *Empire State* which burned in 1887.

EMPIRE STATE

On 13 May 1887 the steamer *Empire State* was berthed at Bristol, Rhode Island for the winter. That evening a fire broke out. The two keepers of the vessel were unable to dowse the flames and narrowly escaped with their lives. In next to no time the *Empire State* was a mass of flames and the wreck sank beneath the water next to the pier.

ULSTER

Human failure rather than human error caused the sinking of the Saugerties Evening Line steamer *Ulster*. On 12 November 1897 she was on the Hudson River with an experienced pilot at the helm. Suddenly he doubled over with stomach cramps and his hands naturally shot off the wheel. In a moment the steamer deviated from course and shot up on to a river bank close to a railroad line. In this position she slowly sank backwards until submerged. But the *Ulster* was not lost. She was later raised and fitted out for her duties on the river. The pilot also recovered.

LEXINGTON

The steamer *Lexington* couldn't have been carrying a worse cargo when she caught fire on 13 January 1840. Her bales of cotton shot flames high into the night sky. Apart from his cargo, Captain George Child had 150 passengers and 40 crewmen on board. Attempts to put out the fire were futile and the captain was unable to beach his stricken vessel. The *Lexington* went down and just four people survived this disaster, one of the worst of the 1840s.

ARMERIA

On 15 August 1897 the steamer *Armeria*, supply vessel to the United States Lighthouse

Above: The steamboat, *Ulster*. Her pilot lost control after an attack of cramps, and grounded the boat.

Below: This lithograph shows the death of the steamer *Lexington*. More than a hundred people lost their lives.

was moving through fog patches in East Penobscot Bay, Maine, when she struck a shelf of rock and rode up on it, in an inadequate imitation of a hovercraft. When the tide went down she presented a strange sight with her stern sticking out of the water. She stayed that way until the 23rd of the month when a host of steamers and tugs hauled her off the rocks and successfully towed her into Northwest Harbor.

MONHEGAN

If a ship can be safe it should be at her slip in port. The *Monhegan* proved a ship is not safe anywhere. Off Dyer Street in Providence, Rhode Island, this steamer, a humble summer tripper, slid out of her slip and sank. A restaurant, four blocks away, found one of her life craft in their door-way. Business was not adversely affected.

Above: The SS Armeria with her stern in the air after she struck rocks.

Below: The SS Monhegan before she slipped her moorings.

Right: The 1882 wreck
of the *Thomas Cornell.*

Above: Debris surrounds
the wreck of the SS
Monhegan at her berth at
Providence after the
hurricane of 1938.

RHODE ISLAND

The steamer *Rhode Island* underwent many changes in her life at sea. Built in 1873, she sailed until 1880 when she was wrecked in Narragansett Bay. By 1882 she had been partly salvaged to become a second *Rhode Island.* Her frame, however, was later used to build a great schooner with six masts, the *Dovrefjeld.* The *Dovrefjeld* was to sink off Staten Island, New York in 1917. Her career didn't end there. She was raised and it wasn't until 1919 that she found her final resting place off Cape Hatteras, North Carolina.

THOMAS CORNELL

Fog again brought about the downfall of the steamer *Thomas Cornell* on 27 March 1882. She was on the Hudson River, moving cautiously, when suddenly she ploughed up on to rocks at Danskammer Point, north of Marlborough, New York. Her bottom was ripped out but later she was pulled off the point and inspected. She was judged unworthy of mending and re-fitting but her frame was used to construct two barges. Such conservation and recycling has always been a part of the shipping industry.

Left: The SS *Bristol* as she was before a saucepan in her galley caused a fire which gutted her.

Right: The SS *Bristol* in the throes of the accident.

Left: The SS *Sultana* taking wood on board.

BRISTOL

The end of one of the finest and most magnificent steamers of the Fall River Line began in a small 'domestic' way. The *Bristol* was built in 1886. She was 2960 tons and contained 240 state rooms, a veritable floating hotel. She was anchored at Newport pier, Rhode Island, on 30 December 1888 when the accident happened: a saucepan of fat caught fire and the fire spread rapidly. She burnt all night and in the morning was gutted.

SULTANA

Estimates vary but it is said that on 21 April 1865 the American paddle steamer *Sultana* was carrying 2394 people, fifty pigs, and a hundred barrels of sugar. The ship's company included Northern prisoners freed at the end of the Civil War, crewmen, passengers, and soldiers. The boilers of the *Sultana* were new but they frequently clogged up. The steamer consequently made many halts.

On 23 April she was near Memphis, off Tagleman's Landing, when the horrific accident occurred. Her boilers blew up and set the ship on fire. Within a short time the vessel was enveloped in flames. Soon afterwards the decks gave way and hundreds of souls sank to their deaths.

There were 741 survivors. Estimates vary as to how many exactly were on the ship (licensed to carry 276) but there is no need to play the numbers game here. Such loss of life from a paddle steamer was unprecedented.

Above: This dramatic woodcut shows the *Sultana* after she exploded; overcrowding contributed to an unprecedented loss of life.

SCHOONERS, BRIGS, AND WINDJAMMERS

Right: The *Henry R Tilton*, wrecked and beached like a toy on Stony Beach in 1897.

THE word schooner originates from the early eighteenth century. It then referred to a fairly small ship with two masts, fore and aft. Like everything else, schooners developed until they had three, four, or even six masts with the wind in their sails. By modern standards they look ancient and vulnerable. In their time they were great and gallant. When we look at them today the beauty of their symmetry seems undeniable. Many were lost but many did their duty of the day.

A brig or brigantine slightly predates a schooner but it is not that different. A brig had a mainmast like a schooner and a foremast. In early days it could also be rowed and was a small vessel. Later the term 'brig' was applied to two-masted sailing vessels in general.

The term 'windjammer' is used in the

Below: The schooner *Messenger* after her encounter with the *Sooloo*.

United States to mean a sailing vessel. The implication was that it was small and doing its best against the elements.

H C HIGGINSON

At eight o'clock on 25 November 1888 the beautiful three-masted schooner *H C Higginson* was caught in a gale from the north-east and ran aground just off Nantasket Beach, Massachusetts. The gale was so fierce that boats from the North Situate station were unable to reach the stricken ship. All would have been lost if it were not for Captain Joshua James of Hull. He and his crew from the Massachusetts Humane Society set out in a life-boat *Nantasket*. They drew alongside the *H C Higginson* and rescued five crewmembers two had already gone over-board and another had frozen to death. They were

Below: Sightseers inspect the wreck of the windjammer *Granite State* near Land's End, England, November 1895. She was destroyed in a storm soon after.

rewarded for their bravery. When the storm abated the schooner was towed into port.

MESSENGER, SOOLOO

On 21 May 1887 seventy miles to the south-east of the South Shoals lightship there was

dense fog at sea. The schooner *Messenger* out of Salem, Massachusetts, ploughed into a vessel, the *Sooloo*, which suffered damage to her masts and superstructure. She was, how-ever, towed into port at Boston where, like many a damaged vessel before her, she was adapted and refitted as a coal barge.

HENRY R TILTON

The brutal gales of November 1898 have gone down in the annals of marine history. The three-masted schooner *Henry R Tilton* is numbered as just one of the many ships wrecked during that period. Fierce winds drove her up on to the beach at Toddy Rocks close to the Point Allerton Life Saving Station which was fortunate for the Tilton's crew of seven. They were all rescued. The schooner was refloated when the storms subsided and she lived to sail again. She finally met her end off Cape Cod in 1912.

MEXICAN

On 17 October 1890 the *Mexican*, a two-masted schooner, was caught in a gale. She was carrying coal from New York City to Bucksport, Maine. She was wrecked in Ipswich Bay, Massachusetts, but her crew of four was saved.

WATER WITCH

The brig *Water Witch* was carrying a cargo of wood when a heavy storm broke and drove the ship up on to the Rhode Island coast on 19 March 1896. Although the vessel was dramatically smashed to pieces the crew were fortunate enough to escape with their lives.

GRANITE STATE

It was a cargo of wheat which finally forced the crew of the American windjammer *Granite State* to abandon ship and launch their boats. The *Granite State* had grounded on rocks, was then hauled off and towed to Portcurno Bay. It was here that the water-logged wheat began to expand and the ship to settle. The crew saved themselves but on 4 November 1895 a storm smashed the sturdy little vessel to nothing more than lengths of firewood.

LOUIS V PLACE

The *Louis V Place*, a three-masted schooner, provides marine history with a grim and

Above: The three-masted schooner *Henry R Tilton* with inspectors on board.

Right: The elegance of the *Sooloo* at sea, before she was plowed into by the *Messenger* in 1887.

solitary tale of survival. During a freezing gale and giant seas this 735-ton vessel on its way from Baltimore to New York became stranded off Long Island close to the Moriches Life Saving Station. The Life Savers were unable to get a boat out to the *Louis V Place* until a whole day had elapsed. Meanwhile the crew of eight had taken to a 'safe' but icy position in the rigging. And it was here that six of the crew died from the cold.

William Stevens and S J Nelson were the two survivors. Stevens was a stalwart soul and was soon laughing and joking that with a good pipe of tobacco and a plate of beans he could have held out much longer. It soon became evident that the same wasn't true of Nelson. He never really recovered from exposure and died soon after his rescue. Such is the strange constitution of different men.

Below: The *Louis V Place* tells a chilling tale of terror.

Right: The brig *Water Witch*, built at Baltimore in 1864, came to a spectacular end in 1896.

POISONED SEAS

EVERY period in maritime history reveals disasters peculiar to the time. Fire and human error will to some degree always be hazards at sea. What has changed, however, is the result of the disaster. This was brought to light by the break-up of the *Torrey Canyon* in March 1967. The sinking of this giant tanker (the 13th largest ship at sea in the world at the time) heralded the birth of the new ecological disaster. Only one human fatality occurred.

The super-tanker was a huge ship, 974 feet long and carrying 117,000 tonnes of oil. She was owned by an American company, flew a Liberian flag, and had an Italian crew under the command of Captain Rugiati. She was

Left: People watch from the Scilly Isles as the *Torrey Canyon* burns.

Above right: Air and sea pollution pour from the crippled tanker.

Right: This side view shows the vast 974-feet-length of the *Torrey Canyon.*

chartered by BP to make a single run from the Persian Gulf to Milford Haven, Wales.

All went well until, approaching the Scilly Isles, the radar showed they were on the port side instead of the starboard. The *Torrey Canyon* was off course. The situation quickly grew complicated. The captain had a deadline to meet. Communication with his chief officer broke down. There were fishing boats in the area. The captain should have reverted from automatic pilot to hand-steering.

In March 1967 the *Torrey Canyon* grounded in the Scilly Isles, a notorious ships' graveyard. She foundered on the Seven Stones Reef and struck the Pollard Rock.

Captain Rugiati's 'Mayday' was immediately picked up by the Dutch salvage tug *Utrecht.* For more than a week the *Utrecht* tried to salvage her prize but without success. Meanwhile oil was drifting on to the shores of Britain. The Royal Navy was finally called in and tried to bomb and ignite the leaking cargo of oil. This too proved unsuccessful. The *Torrey Canyon* broke in half and discharged 50,000 tons of oil which polluted hundreds of miles of British and French coastline. There is really no price which can be put upon a wreck of this kind. Thousands of sea-birds died in the filth as did thousands of fish and other sea life.

Although human error on the part of Captain Rugiati was said to be the cause of the wreck, there was also fierce debate at the time concerning the size of the new super-tanker. Little came of this. The new ecological disaster had arrived and is still with us today.

AMOCO CADIZ

More than a decade after the *Torrey Canyon* disaster the *Amoco Cadiz* smashed up on the rocks of Brittany, France. She discharged more than a quarter million tons of oil, four times the amount of the *Torrey Canyon,* which at the time was seen as the ultimate ecological disaster. Once again the environment was the greatest loser: the Brittany coast-line and marine life suffered. How many similar disasters nature could absorb was a real question of that time, as indeed it remains to this day.

The *Amoco Cadiz* was Spanish-built, owned in the United States, flew a Liberian flag, and was manned by an Italian crew under the command of Captain Bardari.

At 09.46 hours on 16 March 1978 her steering gear ceased to operate. Captain Bardari sent out a message that all ships should therefore keep clear. The *Amoco Cadiz* was gradually heading for the rocky coast of Brittany. The German salvage ship *Pacific* appeared on the scene. The captain wanted a 'towing contract' with the skipper of the *Pacific.* He wanted a 'no cure, no pay' contract. Money was at stake. The exchanges between the two captains were bitter.

In any event the *Pacific's* attempts to tow the *Amoco Cadiz* to safe sea failed as did the dropping of her mighty anchors. She moved in closer and closer to shore until finally she was struck by rocks. Before she broke up the French navy lifted off the crew and their captain.

HAVEN

The *Haven,* sister ship to the *Amoco Cadiz* which went down in 1978, sank in April 1991. She lies a mile and a half off the Italian Riviera. Two explosions left two seamen dead and three posted missing. Others of the crew of 35 were badly burned.

At first the sinking of the Haven with at least 100,000 tonnes of crude oil on board was thought to be the biggest environmental disaster ever. The area, the Bay of Genoa, contains dolphins and the only sperm whales in the Mediterranean. Reports varied and the extent of marine pollution was difficult to gauge. French and Italian authorities said an oil slick 15 miles long and 3 miles wide was being driven along the coast. Roberto Ferrigno of Greenpeace said that the slick was 35 miles long and that it was difficult to believe the authorities when they estimated 40,000 tonnes of oil burnt from the wreck.

The truth of the matter is that, whatever the figures, some oil was pumped out of intact tanks, some was burnt and some taken from the sea, and floundering ashore came birds and marine life trapped in webs of deadly oil, still the most insecure cargo in the 1990s.

Above left and left: The *Amoco Cadiz* goes down, spilling 250,000 tons of oil into the sea.

Above: Fighting the flames of the blazing supertanker *Haven*.

Left: Cleaning up the oil.

75

Right: A tug pulls the supertanker *Exxon Valdez* across Prince William Sound after it was floated off the reef it struck.

Below right: Some sea lions find temporary sanctuary from oily waters.

GLUCKAUF

Perhaps German technology has always been in advance of the rest of the world, because in 1883 the German oil tanker *Gluckauf* was a precursor of our modern supertanker. On 25 March 1883 the *Gluckauf* came to grief in deep fog and beached on Fire Island, New York. All attempts to re-float her failed. The wreck was valued at $125,000 dollars, a staggering figure in those days.

The wreck was stranded in a dramatic port-side position and remained this way for several years. Many tourists came to view this ungainly sight and went away scratching their heads. They weren't to know about marine pollution.

EXXON VALDEZ

On 24 March 1989 the *Exxon Valdez* struck Bligh Reef and poured a quarter of a million barrels of crude oil into the virgin sea off Prince William Sound, Alaska. This was by no means the biggest spill in recent super-tanker history, yet it was the biggest spill in American waters. The United States was outraged. Again the pictures of dying marine life came up on the television screens on both sides of the Atlantic. The feeling was: what can we do and how much battering can the environment take? Will we only know when it's all too late? Real questions and no real answers.

Captain Hazelwood, master of the *Exxon Valdez*, had an excellent record with Exxon's American line of ships. Two things did emerge at the subsequent investigation into this disaster. The Captain's judgment may have been affected by drink and he should have been at the bridge himself when nego-tiating the bergs around Bligh Reef. He was, however, cleared of criminal negligence.

ARGO MERCHANT

Another oil tanker which came to grief was the *Argo Merchant*, owned, to quote the Liberian Board of Investigation, by 'New York Greeks.' The *Argo Merchant* had a history of mishaps and it seems remarkable that she lasted so long.

She was on a passage from Venezuela to Boston when her position in relation to the Nantucket lightship became highly con-fused. The captain was later to claim that according to readings the lightship was ahead when in fact she was astern. The fact of the matter was that they had lost their position and failed to take necessary precautionary measures.

The *Argo Merchant* came aground on Fish-ing Rip Shoal, about thirty miles north of the

lightship. She didn't at first break up. Prompt action by tugs might have saved her. No such action was taken. The weather took a turn for the worse and smashed the old tanker up. 25,000 tons of oil poured into the rich fishing area off Cape Cod. Only a heavy wind from the west saved these fishing grounds from major pollution. Consequently the *Argo Merchant* drew attention not so much to marine pollution but to the sub-standard tankers at sea making a dangerous fast buck.

Above: The tanker *Argo Merchant* aground off New England.

Above right: A spectacular aerial shot of the broken tanker *Amoco Cadiz.*

Right: The weather takes a turn for the worse and breaks up the supertanker *Argo Merchant.*

Top: Oil from the *Exxon Valdez* is pumped aboard the *Exxon Baton Rouge* in the clean-up operation.

Above: In the Port of Valdez oil is cleaned off fishing boats which fish in Prince William Sound.

Left: The oily beach on Smith Island is hosed by sea water. Later it is skimmed off the sea.

INDEX

Figures in *italics*
refer to illustrations

Alva Cape, tanker 32,
 32, 33
Amoco Cadiz, tanker 72,
 73
Andrea Doria, liner
 30-32, *30, 31*
Antarctic exploration
 16, *16*
Argo Merchant, tanker
 76-77, *78*
Ariadne, yacht 46, *46*
Armeria, steamer 58-59,
 59
Atlantique, L', liner *34*

Ballard, Robert 6, 10, *11*
Bardari, Captain 72
Beaudean, Captain
 Raoul 31
Berlitz, Charles 20
Bermuda Triangle
 19-20, *19*, 21-24
Bowbelle, dredger 26, 28
Briggs, Captain
 Benjamin Spooner *25*
SS *Bristol*, steamer *62*,
 63
Bustler, tug 20

Calamai, Captain Piero
 30
calentura 45-46
Cardinal Vertue, yacht 45
Carlsen, Captain 17
Carol Deering 23
Carpathia 12, 13, 14
Cepheus, steamer 56
Chichester, Sir Francis
 43, 44, *44*
City of Columbus,
 steamer 53, *53*
SS *City of Guildford* 34
Cobequid, steamer *51*
Columbia, steamship *50*
Compass, Liberty ship 43
Coutwood, Captain 30
HMS *Curacoa*, cruiser
 28, 30
USS *Cyclops*, collier *20*,
 21, 22

Dei Gratia, brigantine
 24, *25*
Dexterous, tug 20
Dona Paz, ferry *26*
Dovrefjeld, schooner 60

Eastland, steamer 53-54,
 53, 54, 55

ecological disasters 70,
 70-71, 72, *73-79*,
 76-77
Emmeline, steamer
 56-57, *56*
Empire State, steamer
 57, 58
Endurance, exploration
 vessel 16, *16*
Exxon Valdez, tanker
 76, *76-77*, *79*

Fastnet Race 44 1979 *45*,
 46, 46
Ferret, piracy of 18
Flying Enterprise, cargo
 ship 17, *17*

Gate City, steamer 56
General Slocum,
 steamboat 50-52, *51*,
 52
Gipsy Moth IV, yacht
 43, 44, *44*
Gloria Colite, schooner
 24
Gluckauf, tanker 76
Grandcamp, freighter 38,
 40, *40*
Granite State,
 windjammer *66*, 68
Great Eastern, steamship
 50

H C Higginson,
 schooner 64, 66
Haven, tanker 72, *73*,
 74, 75
Hazelwood, Captain 76
Henderson, Captain 28
Henry R Tilton,
 schooner 65, *66-67*,
 68
Herald of Free Enterprise,
 ferry *2-3*, 47, *47, 48*,
 49
SS *High Flyer*, freighter
 40

Ile de France 31
Illingworth, Captain 30
Iroquois, steamer *56, 57*
Ismay, J Bruce 12, 13

James, Captain Joshua
 64
João Costa 44
John and Mary 23
John H Starin, steamer
 57

Knorr, US Navy
 research ship 6

Lewis, Dr David 44-45
Lexington, steamer 58,

58
liners 6, *6-15*, 10-14, 28,
 28-31, 30-32, *34, 40*,
 41, *41*
Lloyds of London 18, *18*
Louis V Place, schooner
 68-69, *69*
Lusitania, liner 14, *14, 15*

Macfarlane, Captain R
 D 36
Maine, steamer 56
Marchioness, pleasure
 boat 26, 27, 28, *28*
Mary Celeste, brigantine
 24-25, *24, 25*
Messenger, schooner *64*,
 65
Mexican, schooner 67
Monhegan, steamer 59,
 59, 60
Morehouse, Captain
 David 24-25
Morro Castle, passenger
 ship 36, 37-38, *37*

Nordenson, Captain
 Gunnar 30
Normandie, liner *40*, 41,
 41
SS *Noronic*, pleasure
 cruiser 38, *38, 39*
Norumbega, steamboat
 56, 57

oil spillage 70, *70-71*,
 72, *73-79*, *76-77*
Olympic, liner 6, 10
Oostmeer, cargo ship 19

Pacific, salvage ship 72
Parker, Captain Gilman
 25
SS *Portsea 34*, 36

Queen Mary, liner 28,
 28, 29, 30

Rhode Island, steamer
 4-5, 60, *61*
Rostrom, Captain
 Arthur H 13
Royal George 49, 49
Rubicon, Cuban ship
 22
Rugiati, Captain 70, 72

São Paulo, battleship 20,
 43
Scandanavian Star, ferry
 35
Shackleton, Sir Ernest
 16, *16*
Slocum, Joshua 45-46
Smith, Captain Edward
 J 11, 12, *12*, 13-14, *13*

Sooloo 64, 66, 68
Stockholm, liner 30-31,
 31
SS Marine *Sulphur
 Queen* cargo ship
 21-23, *21, 22, 23*
SS *Sultana*, paddle
 steamer 62, 63, *63*

tankers 21-23, *23*, 32,
 32-33, 70, *70-71*, 72,
 73-79, *76-77*
Tenacious, yacht *45*, 46,
 46
SS *Texaco Massachusetts*
 tanker 32, *32*
Thomas Cornell, steamer

60, *61*
Titanic, liner 6, *6*, 8, *9*,
 10-14, *10, 11, 12, 13*, 43
Torrey Canyon, tanker
 70, *70*, 71, 72
Turner, Captain
 William 14, *14*

Ulster, steamer 58, *58*

Washington, steamship
 50
Water Witch, brig 68, *69*
World War I 14, 21
World War II 28, 36, 41

yachts *43-46*, *44-46*

ACKNOWLEDGMENTS

The publisher would like to than Casebourne
Rose, who designed this book, and the following
agencies for supplying the illustrations:

Associated Press: page 71 (below)

Associated Press/Worldwide Photos Inc: pages
11 (below), 75 (below), 78 (above)

Beken Photographic, Cowes, Isle of Wight:
pages 45, 46 (both)

The Bettmann Archive: pages 1, 2-3, 10-11
(Woods Hole Oceanographic Institute), 14 (both),
15 (below and left), 16 (both), 17, 34, 36 (both),
37 (above), 50, 51 (both), 53 (below), 54 (both),
55 (above), 58 (below), 63

Bettmann/Hulton: page 13 (above)

J Allan Cash Ltd: page 44

Frank E Claes, Ship Photos and Research: page
56 (both), 59 (above), 60, 61 (top), 68 (both), 69
(both)

The Mansell Collection: pages 24, 25 (top and
left)

The National Maritime Museum, Greenwich:
pages 15 (above), 49

The Peabody Museum of Salem: pages 4-5, 8-9,
25 (bottom), 53 (above), 56 (center), 57, 58
(above), 59 (below), 61 (both), 62 (center and
below), 64, 65, 66-67

Reuters/Bettmann: pages 26, 27 (both), 28
(above), 35 (both), 47 (both), 48-49, 73, 77
(below), 79 (bottom right and bottom left)

Donald C Ringwald Marine Collection Ltd:
pages 56 (top: Brundige Photo)

**The Titanic Historical Society, Indian
 Orchard, MA:** pages 6 (above, Ray Lepian
Collection), 8 (Ulster Folk and Transport
Museum), 9 (Ray Lepian Collection), 12 (above,
courtesy of George Behe Collection)

UPI/Bettmann: pages 13 (below), 17 (below), 18,
19 (both), 20, 21, 22 (both), 23 (both)